# THE 12 MOST AMAZING
## AMERICAN MONUMENTS & SYMBOLS

by Anita Yasuda

12 STORY LIBRARY

www.12StoryLibrary.com

12-Story Library is an imprint of Peterson Publishing Company and Press Room Editions.

Produced for 12-Story Library by Red Line Editorial

Photographs ©: Richard A McMillin/Shutterstock Images, cover, 1; NASA, 4; eurobanks/ Shutterstock Images, 5; Chawalit S/Shutterstock Images, 6; Massimo Colombo/Shutterstock Images, 7; Bildagentur Zoonar GmbH/Shutterstock Images, 8, 28; indigolotos/Shutterstock Images, 9; Jimmy May/AP Images, 10; Harris & Ewing/Library of Congress, 11, 23; Orhan Cam/Shutterstock Images, 12, 13, 24; Carol M. Highsmith/Library of Congress, 14, 16, 29; Mark Krapels/Shutterstock Images, 15; Library of Congress, 17, 18; Thomas Nast/Library of Congress, 19; ExaMedia Photography/Shutterstock Images, 20; Vizual Studio/Shutterstock Images, 21; Andrew B. Graham/Library of Congress, 22; Anthony Correia/Shutterstock Images, 25; trekandshoot/Shutterstock Images, 26; Gary716/Shutterstock Images, 27

**ISBN**
978-1-63235-009-1 (hardcover)
978-1-63235-069-5 (paperback)
978-1-62143-050-6 (hosted ebook)

**Library of Congress Control Number: 2014937242**

Printed in the United States of America
Mankato, MN
June, 2014

Go beyond the book. Get free, up-to-date content on this topic at 12StoryLibrary.com.

# TABLE OF CONTENTS

# AMERICAN FLAG REPRESENTS UNITY, PATRIOTISM

Only one country's flag flies on the moon. US astronaut Buzz Aldrin planted the American flag in 1969 during the first moon landing. Here on Earth, American flags have been flying since June 14, 1777. On that day, the Continental Congress approved a design with 13 stars and 13 stripes. They represented the 13 colonies, which became the first 13 states in the new union.

The first American flag left on the moon was blown over during takeoff, but five flags from later missions are still standing.

The 50-star version of the flag has been in use for more than 50 years.

No one is sure who designed the first flag. According to one popular legend, George Washington asked seamstress Betsy Ross to make it. Francis Hopkinson, a member of the Continental Congress, also took credit for the design. He even asked Congress for payment.

The flag design has been altered over the years, but it still has 13 stripes to represent the colonies. The number of stars has grown as new states have joined the United States. The flag now has 50 stars. The last star was added for Hawaii in 1960.

## 3,000

Weight in pounds (1,400 kg) of the largest US flag. In 1996, it was hung across the Hoover Dam.

- Flag design approved on June 14, 1777.
- Inspired Francis Scott Key to write "The Star-Spangled Banner" in 1814.
- National Flag Day is celebrated on June 14.
- Nicknames: "Stars and Stripes" and "Old Glory"

## EARLY FLAGS

During the American Revolution, many different symbols were used on flags flown by the colonists who were fighting the British. The soldiers' flags represented ideas such as home, freedom, or bravery. One flag featured pine trees. Others had animals, such as beavers or snakes. One version had an anchor on it.

# 2

# STATUE OF LIBERTY STANDS TALL FOR FREEDOM

The Statue of Liberty rises 15 stories high in the New York Harbor. For more than 125 years, it has welcomed visitors and immigrants to the United States. At night, light from the statue's torch can be seen up to 24 miles (39 km) away.

The statue was a gift from France to the United States. It was a sign of friendship between the countries. French sculptor Frédéric-Auguste Bartholdi began work on it in 1875. His team hammered copper sheets into shape by hand. In 1885, the statue was ready to be delivered to the United States. It was so big that it had to be split into 350 pieces to be loaded onto a ship. Workers spent four months putting it back together after it got to New York.

The Statue of Liberty stands on Liberty Island, which also includes a museum.

Visitors to the Statue of Liberty can climb to the top of the pedestal or all the way to the crown.

On October 28, 1886, President Grover Cleveland dedicated the Statue of Liberty. Since then, it has been one of the country's most recognizable symbols of freedom and democracy. The statue also became important to immigrants arriving in the United States. Approximately 14 million immigrants entered the country through New York between 1886 and 1924. Many saw the Statue of Liberty as a symbol of freedom, opportunity, and hope.

## 377
### Stairs visitors climb to reach the crown.

- Statue and pedestal measure 305 feet (93 m).
- Located on Liberty Island in Upper New York Bay.
- Restored in 1986.
- Approximately 4 million visitors per year.

## THINK ABOUT IT

Symbols can mean different things to different people. What do you think of when you see the image of the Statue of Liberty?

# AMERICAN BALD EAGLE FLIES AS NATIONAL BIRD

When it was founded in 1776, the United States did not have an official seal. A national seal is a symbol that is used on important documents. It took Congress six years to decide what the country's seal should look like. They wanted to find an image that would make Americans proud.

The United States has more than 10,000 nesting pairs of bald eagles.

# 2007

**Year bald eagles were taken off the endangered list.**

- Became the national bird on June 20, 1782.
- Only lives in North America.
- Protected from hunting since 1940.

Some people wanted to use the rattlesnake. The rattlesnake had appeared on flags during the American Revolution. Others argued for the dove or the rooster. In 1782, Congress approved the American bald eagle as the national bird. A newly created national seal featured the bird. It also began to appear on coins, paper money, and stamps.

Benjamin Franklin, one of the founding fathers, did not think this was a good idea. He said the eagle lacked courage because it fled from smaller birds. But others saw the eagle as a symbol of strength, long life, and liberty. According to one story, the noise from one of the early battles of the American Revolution woke up some eagles nearby. They flew over the battlefield, shrieking. Colonial soldiers thought they were calling out for freedom.

The seal featuring the bald eagle can be seen on a dollar bill.

9

# "STAR-SPANGLED BANNER" BECOMES NATIONAL ANTHEM

In 1812, the United States went to war against Great Britain over trade and territory issues. It was a bold move. The British navy was the largest in the world. The United States would have to hold off a naval attack to win the war. On the night of September 13, 1814, a battle began at Fort McHenry in Baltimore, Maryland. British ships began firing on the fort. All night long, the sky lit up with cannon fire. A lawyer named Francis Scott Key watched the battle from a ship in the bay.

The next morning, Key saw that the US troops had held off the British. The American flag still flew above the fort. Key was so inspired by the sight that he wrote a poem. Soon, newspapers began

Americans stand and remove their hats when "The Star-Spangled Banner" is being played.

10

## 117

Years after Key's song was written that it became the official national anthem.

- Became the official song for the US military in 1916.
- Played at the World Series to honor troops serving in World War I in 1918.
- Became the official national anthem in 1931.

## THE FLAG

Mary Pickersgill was a Baltimore seamstress who made flags in the early 1800s. In 1813, she sewed a flag for Fort McHenry. This is the flag that Francis Scott Key saw the night he wrote the poem. The original flag made by Pickersgill is on display at the Smithsonian National Museum of American History.

printing his poem. Key later set it to music. He used an English song for the melody. By the late 1800s, the song had become well known.

In 1931, Congress voted to make "The Star-Spangled Banner" the national anthem.

The poem written by Francis Scott Key was originally called "The Defence of Fort McHenry."

# WHITE HOUSE BUILT AS SEAT OF POWER

In 1792, President George Washington decided to have a contest to design the presidential home. Washington wanted a building that would command respect for the newly formed country. He also wanted a classic design that would stand the test of time. In the end, Irish architect James Hoban won with his simple vision for the White House.

In 1800, the second US president, John Adams, became the first to live in the White House. Adams's wife, Abigail, was not impressed. She thought the unfinished home looked like a barn. By the time James Madison moved into the White House in 1809, the home was ready. Madison was president during the War of 1812, between Britain and the United States. The British attacked the White House and set it on fire. Afterward, only the outside walls were left. James Monroe moved into the rebuilt White House in 1817.

It takes 570 gallons (2,160 L) of paint to keep the outside of the White House looking pristine.

## RENOVATIONS

Many presidents have decided to improve or add on to the White House. President Theodore Roosevelt had the West Wing built in 1902. He wanted to separate the home and office spaces in the White House. The Oval Office was constructed in 1909, after William Taft had taken office. The White House tennis court was moved to make room for it. In 1942, a cloakroom was converted into a movie theater. President Richard Nixon had a one-lane bowling alley installed underground in 1969.

Now, more than 6,000 people visit the home at 1600 Pennsylvania Avenue each day. The building has changed much over the years. But to many, it has always been a monument to history and leadership in the United States.

## 132
### Rooms in the White House residence.

- Constructed between 1792 and 1800.
- Has been known as the President's Palace, the President's House, and the Executive Mansion.
- Called the White House beginning in 1901.

The south portico of the White House was added in 1830.

# CRACKED LIBERTY BELL BROUGHT COUNTRY TOGETHER

The Liberty Bell doesn't make a sound. But millions of people visit Philadelphia to see it each year. In 1751, colonists in Pennsylvania decided they wanted a bell for their assembly hall. When finished, it weighed more than 2,000 pounds (900 kg). The bell was cast in London. After it arrived, the bell cracked before it could even be hung in the assembly hall. A new bell was cast in Pennsylvania, using metal from the original.

A message was carved onto the bell. It said, "Proclaim liberty throughout the land unto all the inhabitants thereof." Pennsylvanians rang the bell for many occasions.

The Liberty Bell is mostly made of copper and tin, with small amounts of other metals.

## SAFEKEEPING

During the American Revolution, the Liberty Bell was taken down from the assembly house. Pennsylvanians did not want it to fall into British hands. The bell was hidden under a church floor. It was returned to the city in 1778.

The Liberty Bell is on display in Independence National Historical Park in Philadelphia.

The bell called people to hear the first reading of the Declaration of Independence on July 8, 1776. It cracked again in 1835. It was being rung for the funeral of Supreme Court Chief Justice John Marshall.

The crack grew when it was rung for George Washington's birthday in 1846. The bell could not be used again without damaging it even more. But it became an important symbol during the Civil War. People who wanted to end slavery called it the Liberty Bell. After the Civil War, the bell toured the country. It had become a symbol of unity between the North and South.

## 24.5
### Length in inches (62.2 cm) of the Liberty Bell's crack.

- First cast in 1752 in London.
- Recast in 1753.
- First called the Liberty Bell in the 1830s.

15

# MOUNT RUSHMORE HONORS FOUR PRESIDENTS

It took approximately 400 men and women 14 years to carve the faces on Mount Rushmore. They worked whether it was hot, cold, raining, or snowing. Each day, the workers climbed 700 steps. Then they were strapped into seats, which were lowered down the mountainside by steel cables. They used dynamite to blast the face of the mountain. Then they used jackhammers, chisels, and drills to carve the details.

The idea for the monument came from state historian Doane Robinson. He wanted South Dakota to have a big attraction. He hoped more people would visit

Mount Rushmore is the world's largest sculpture.

# 60

Height in feet (18 m) of each president's face.

- Built from October 4, 1927, to October 31, 1941.
- Located in South Dakota.
- Made of granite.
- Features presidents George Washington, Thomas Jefferson, Theodore Roosevelt, and Abraham Lincoln.

the state. Designer Gutzon Borglum suggested featuring four presidents who were important to US history: George Washington, Thomas Jefferson, Abraham Lincoln, and Theodore Roosevelt. Washington and Jefferson were chosen to represent the country's founding and expansion. Lincoln was featured for keeping the country united. Roosevelt was chosen for his role in turning the United States into a global power.

The monument's site in the Black Hills National Forest has made it controversial. The Black Hills are sacred to the Lakota Sioux.

Gutzon Borglum and another worker inspect George Washington's nose in 1932.

But white settlers forced them to leave in the 1800s. To many Native Americans, Mount Rushmore still represents the Europeans' unjust treatment of them from this time period.

# 8

## UNCLE SAM STANDS FOR US GOVERNMENT

Before Uncle Sam stood for the US government, he was a real person. Samuel Wilson lived in Troy, New York. Wilson sold meat to the US Army in the War of 1812. He put the letters "U.S." on his

NAVY!

Uncle Sam is calling YOU ENLIST in the Navy!

Recruiting Station.

"I WANT YOU IN THE NAVY and I WANT YOU NOW"

The military used Uncle Sam on recruitment posters.

# 1813

Year a newspaper first used the term "Uncle Sam."

- Based on Samuel Wilson.
- Used on army recruiting posters starting in 1917.
- Congress recognized Wilson as the man behind Uncle Sam in 1961.

Thomas Nast drew this cartoon of Uncle Sam in 1877.

barrels. People joked that the "U.S." stood for "Uncle Sam." The story caught on, and the nickname came to represent the US government.

The character of Uncle Sam soon appeared in cartoon drawings. Artist Thomas Nast drew cartoons in the 1860s and 1870s. He drew Uncle Sam wearing a suit in the colors of the American flag. Sometimes he had on a cap and a nightshirt in stars and stripes. Another well-known image of Uncle Sam was created by James Montgomery Flagg. He painted Uncle Sam with a top hat and white beard. In 1917, the US Army used this image on a poster. Under the image of Uncle Sam, the poster said "I Want You for the U.S. Army!" Since then, Uncle Sam has been featured in many newspapers, songs, and advertisements.

# WASHINGTON MONUMENT RISES ABOVE NATION'S CAPITAL

The Washington Monument is the world's tallest free-standing stone structure. Its 36,000 stones are not held together by mortar or cement. The stones are held in place by their own weight. The elevator ride to the

The Washington Monument overlooks the National Mall, which includes other monuments and a reflecting pool.

# 55

**Width in feet (17 m) of the monument at its base.**

- Built between 1848 and 1884.
- Designed by Robert Mills.
- Opened on February 21, 1885.
- Honors President George Washington.

The Washington Monument is the world's tallest obelisk. An obelisk is a four-sided column that tapers to a point at the top.

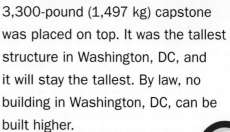

top gives visitors a view of the city 500 feet (150 m) below. From the top, visitors can see the White House, the Lincoln Memorial, the Pentagon, and many other landmarks of Washington, DC. They even can see parts of Virginia and Maryland.

At first, a group of citizens funded the monument's construction. Work began in 1848. But money soon ran out. For 20 years, the unfinished monument stood at 156 feet (47.5 m). Some said it looked like a broken chimney. In 1876, the US government decided to take over the project.

In 1884, a big crowd gathered below the monument. They watched as its

3,300-pound (1,497 kg) capstone was placed on top. It was the tallest structure in Washington, DC, and it will stay the tallest. By law, no building in Washington, DC, can be built higher.

21

# GREAT SEAL DESIGNED TO REPRESENT THE NATION

On July 4, 1776, the American colonies declared their independence from Great Britain. The Continental Congress decided that the new nation needed a seal. They wanted it to be a strong symbol of the United States. Three groups met over the years. None could come to a decision. Charles Thompson then looked at all of the groups' designs. He was the secretary of Congress.

Instead of picking, Thompson used ideas from each of the groups. He designed a seal that had a large eagle in the center. It looked like it was rising up in the air. On its chest was a bold red and white shield. The eagle held an olive branch and arrows. The reverse side of the seal

The olive branch and the arrows on the Great Seal represent peace and war.

## THINK ABOUT IT

If you were designing a seal for the United States, what would your design include? What if you were designing a seal for your school or for your family?

# 13

**Number of stripes on the seal's shield, to represent the original 13 colonies.**

- Approved by Congress on June 20, 1782.
- Only the secretary of state can give permission to use the Great Seal.
- Includes a Latin phrase, *e pluribus unum,* that means "out of many, one."

had a pyramid. This image can be seen on the back of the one dollar bill. On June 20, 1782, Congress approved his design.

The tool that is used to imprint the Great Seal on documents is called a die. The die for the Great Seal is kept in the Department of State. The design is stamped on approximately 3,000 official documents each year. The seal's design is also used on everything from stamps to coins to passports. It can be seen on military buttons and buildings, too.

A state department employee uses a die to imprint the Great Seal onto documents.

# LINCOLN MEMORIAL IMPORTANT TO CIVIL RIGHTS MOVEMENT

The south wall of the Lincoln Memorial contains the words from President Abraham Lincoln's Gettysburg Address. His second inaugural address is etched on the north wall. Another famous speech is also connected to the Lincoln Memorial. Civil rights leader Martin Luther King Jr. gave the "I Have a Dream" speech here in 1963. Approximately 200,000 people gathered to hear King's speech at the end of the March for Jobs and Freedom. It was 100 years after

Construction of the Lincoln Memorial took eight years.

The statue of Lincoln is sculpted from white marble.

the Gettysburg Address. The Lincoln Memorial also was the site of many other civil rights demonstrations.

The design of the Lincoln Memorial was based on the Parthenon, a temple in Greece. It has 36 marble columns. They stand for the 36 states at the time of Lincoln's death in 1865. Inside, a 19-foot (6-m) statue of Lincoln sits. One of his hands is open, and the other is closed in a fist. This was meant to represent strength and compassion. The memorial was dedicated in 1922.

# 175

**Weight in tons (160 t) of the statue of Lincoln.**

- Built from 1914 to 1922.
- Designed by Henry Bacon.
- Marble statue of Lincoln made by Daniel Chester French.
- Jules Guerin painted the murals, which stand for freedom and unity.

## GETTYSBURG ADDRESS

Lincoln gave the Gettysburg Address on November 19, 1863. He delivered it on the Pennsylvania battlefield where the Battle of Gettysburg was fought. The speech was only 273 words long. But it is remembered for its support of equality and freedom.

# US CAPITOL BUILDING COMMANDS RESPECT

The Capitol Building is where Congress makes new laws. It is so big that the Statue of Liberty could fit inside its white dome. The building has more than 600 rooms and miles of halls. It even has a small subway to help people get around. In 2008, a new visitor's center opened. The Capitol welcomes more than 3 million people each year.

The Capitol was built on a high area of land. It is called Capitol Hill, or just the Hill. But it wasn't much more than a field in the 1700s. George Washington chose the site. A contest was held to pick a design. William Thornton, a medical doctor and part-time architect, won.

The design of the Capitol was inspired by ancient Greek and Roman buildings.

# 9 million

Weight in tons (8.2 million t) of the Capitol dome.

- Site selected in 1791.
- Designed by William Thornton.
- Houses the US Senate and House of Representatives.

In 1793, work on the Capitol Building started. Construction has continued off and on for more than 200 years.

It was rebuilt after a fire during the War of 1812 and again after a fire in 1898. At other times, it was expanded. During the Civil War, it was used to house troops. Rooms were filled with their baggage and food. The basement became a bakery. Its 20 ovens filled the Library of Congress with smoke. In modern times, the Capitol also serves as a museum of art and history. Paintings and sculptures show important events from US history.

The Capitol dome has 108 windows.

# FACT SHEET

- The Antiquities Act was passed in 1906. It gives the president and Congress the authority to create national monuments on federal land. A national monument is defined as land set aside by the federal government to protect an important site or landmark.

- In 1906, Devils Tower in Wyoming became the first US national monument, under President Theodore Roosevelt. Roosevelt created 28 national monuments, more than any president to date.

- Since 1906, presidents have designated 128 national monuments. Some pieces of land that were made into monuments were later changed to national parks. The Grand Canyon, the Petrified Forest, and Lassen Peak were national monuments that later became parks.

- Presidents have also used the Antiquities Act to enlarge monuments. For example, President Lyndon B. Johnson added Ellis Island to the Statue of Liberty National Monument in 1965.

- As of 2014, President Barack Obama had established five new monuments, including the Harriet Tubman Underground Railroad in Maryland.

- Periodically, national monuments need to be restored. From 1982 to 1986, the Statue of Liberty was restored by a joint French-American team. They repaired damage to Liberty's copper skin. They also replaced the torch, which had been damaged by water. The new torch is covered in 24-karat gold sheets.

- The Statue of Liberty has appeared in many movies and television shows. In 1983, magician David Copperfield performed an illusion in which the statue disappeared.

- Many monuments and symbols such as the American bald eagle, Statue of Liberty, and Mount Rushmore have been featured on US currency.

# GLOSSARY

**architect**
A person who designs buildings.

**capital**
A city that is the center
of government.

**Civil War**
A war fought between Northern
and Southern US states from 1861
to 1865.

**colony**
An area that is controlled by another
country that is far away.

**Congress**
The branch of the US government
that passes laws.

**democracy**
A form of government in which
people choose leaders by voting.

**granite**
A hard stone used for building.

**immigrant**
A person who comes to a country to
live there.

**independence**
Freedom from control, such as from
another country.

**landmark**
A building or place that is easily
recognizable or important to history.

**monument**
A building designed to honor a
person, event, or idea.

**pedestal**
A base for a statue.

**seal**
A symbol that represents a country
and is pressed on important
government papers.

**symbol**
A letter, picture, or object that
represents something else.

# FOR MORE INFORMATION

## Books

House, Katherine L. *The White House for Kids: A History of a Home, Office, and National Symbol*. Chicago: Chicago Review Press, 2014.

Kent, Deborah. *The Statue of Liberty*. New York: Scholastic, 2012.

McHugh, Erin. *National Parks: A Kid's Guide to America's Parks, Monuments, and Landmarks*. New York: Black Dog & Leventhal, 2012.

Niver, Heather Moore. *20 Fun Facts about US Monuments*. New York: Gareth Stevens, 2013.

Spier, Peter. *The Star-Spangled Banner*. New York: Doubleday, 2014.

## Websites

Ben's Guide to US Government for Kids
bensguide.gpo.gov

National Park Service
www.nps.gov

Smithsonian: The Star-Spangled Banner
amhistory.si.edu/starspangledbanner

# INDEX

## About the Author

Anita Yasuda is the author of more than 80 books for children. She enjoys writing biographies, books about science, social studies, and chapter books. She lives in Huntington Beach, California.

## READ MORE FROM 12-STORY LIBRARY

Every 12-Story Library book is available in many formats, including Amazon Kindle and Apple iBooks. For more information, visit your device's store or 12StoryLibrary.com.